Impressum
Verlag: BABADADA GmbH, Nedderfeld 112 , 22529 Hamburg
Geschäftsführer / Verlagsleitung: Harald Hof
Druck: Books on Demand GmbH, In de Tarpen 42, 22848 Norderstedt

Imprint
Publisher: BABADADA GmbH, Nedderfeld 112 , 22529 Hamburg, Germany
Managing Director / Publishing direction: Harald Hof
Print: Books on Demand GmbH, In de Tarpen 42, 22848 Norderstedt

school

paaralan

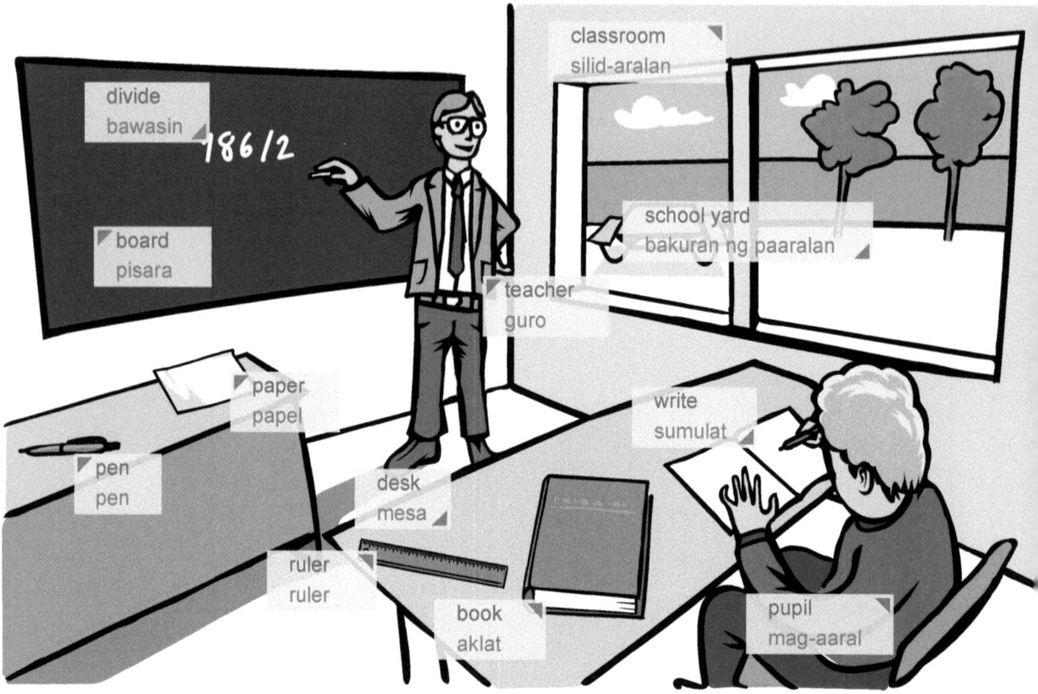

classroom
silid-aralan
divide
bawasin
186/2
board
pisara
school yard
bakuran ng paaralan
teacher
guro
paper
papel
write
sumulat
pen
pen
desk
mesa
ruler
ruler
book
aklat
pupil
mag-aaral

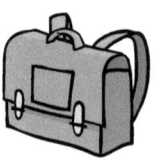

satchel
satchel

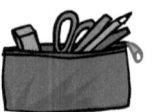

pencil case
lalagyan ng lapis

pencil
lapis

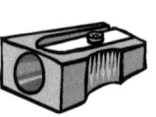

pencil sharpener
pantasa

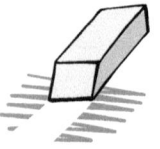

rubber
goma

drawing pad
drowing pad

drawing

drowing

paintbrush

pinsel na pampinta

paint box

kahon ng pinta

scissors

gunting

glue

pandikit

exercise book

aklat para sa pagsasanay

homework

takdang-aralin

number

numero

add

dagdagan

subtract

bawasin

multiply

paramihin

calculate

kalkulahin

letter

liham

alphabet

alpabeto

word

salita

text
teksto

read
basahin

chalk
yeso

lesson
leksyon

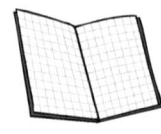
register
rehistro

examination
eksaminasyon

certificate
sertipiko

school uniform
uniporme sa paaralan

education
edukasyon

encyclopedia
encyclopedia

university
unibersidad

microscope
mikroskopyo

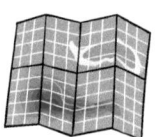
map
mapa

waste-paper basket
basurahan ng papel

travel

paglalakbay

hotel
hotel
Grand
hostel
hostel
ROOMS
currency exchange office
tanggapan ng palitan ng pera
car
kotse

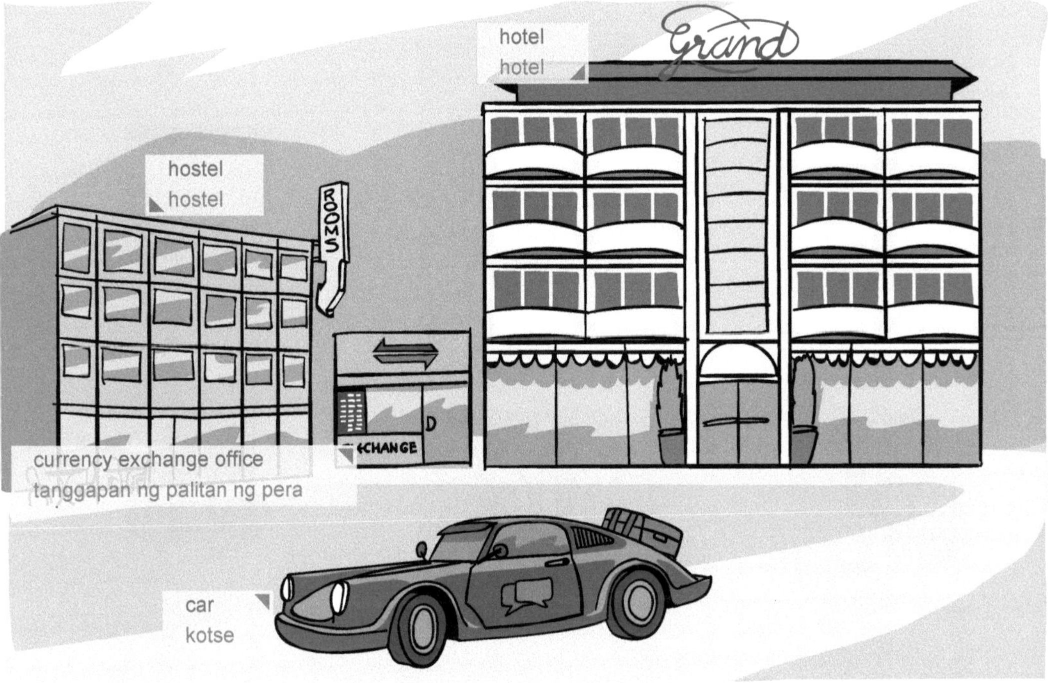

language
wika

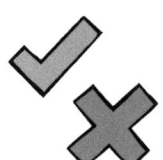

yes / no
oo / hindi

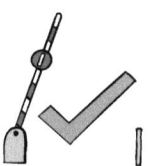

Okay
Okey

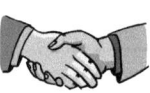

hello
kumusta

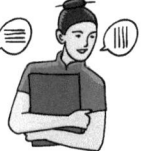

translator
tagapagsalin

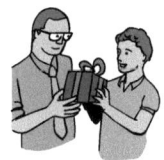

Thank you
Salamat

how much is...?

magkano ang...?

I don't get it

Hindi ko maintindihan

problem

problema

Good evening!

Magandang gabi!

Good morning!

Magandang umaga!

Good night!

Magandang gabi!

goodbye

paalam

direction

direksyon

luggage

bahage

bag

bag

backpack

napsak

guest

panauhin

room

silid

sleeping bag

sakong tulugan

tent

tolda

tourist information

impormasyon ng turista

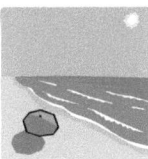

beach

dalampasigan

credit card

credit card

breakfast

almusal

lunch

tanghalian

dinner

hapunan

Ticket

tiket

elevator

elebeytor

stamp

selyo

border

hangganan

customs

adwana

embassy

embahada

visa

visa

passport

pasaporte

transport
transportasyon

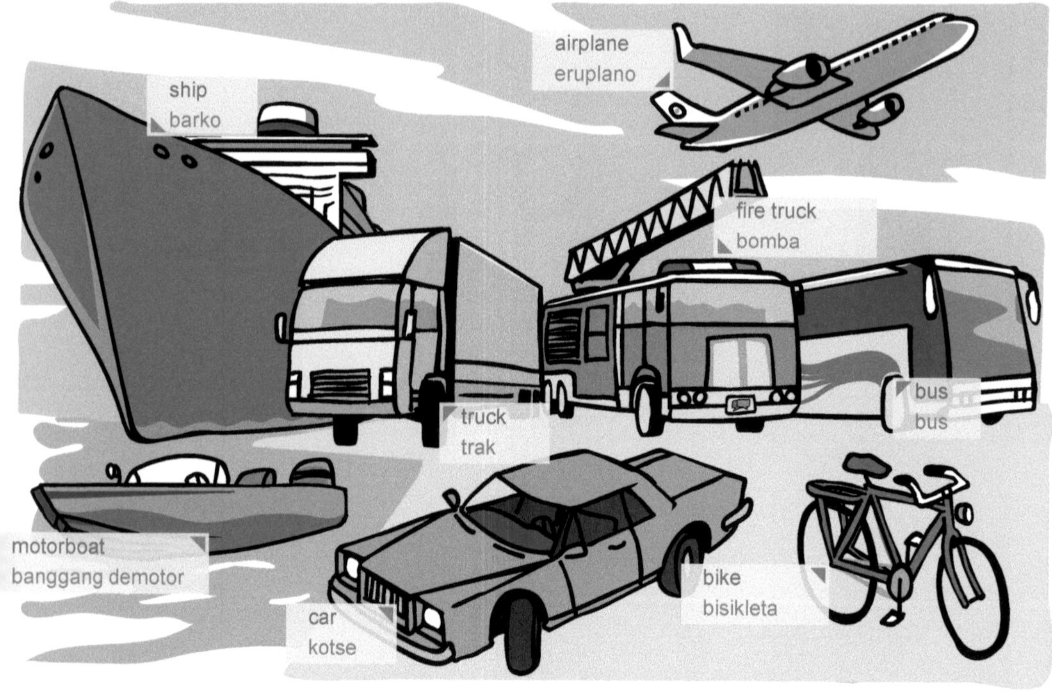

airplane
eruplano
ship
barko
fire truck
bomba
bus
bus
truck
trak
motorboat
banggang demotor
bike
bisikleta
car
kotse

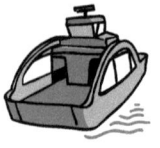

ferry

lantsang pantawid

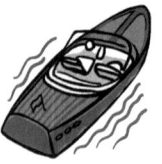

boat

bangka

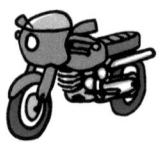

motorbike

motorsiklo

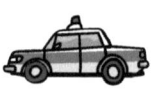

police car

sasakyan ng pulis

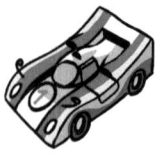

racing car

kotseng pangkarera

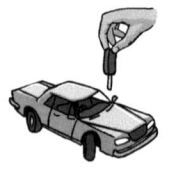

rental car

nirerentahang kotse

car sharing

car sharing

tow truck

trak na panghila

garbage truck

trak na pantapon ng basura

engine

motor

fuel

panggatong

fuel station

gasolinahan

traffic sign

karatula ng trapiko

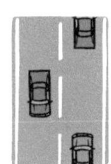

traffic

trapiko

traffic jam

masikip na trapiko

parking lot

paradahan ng kotse

train station

estasyon ng tren

tracks

riles

train

tren

tram

trambya

wagon

wagon

helicopter

helikopter

airport

paliparan

tower

tore

passenger

pasahero

container

sisidlan

carton

karton

cart

kariton

basket

basket

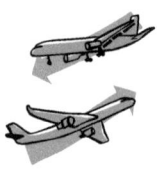

take off / land

umalis / lumapag

village

nayon

city center

sentro ng lungsod

house

bahay

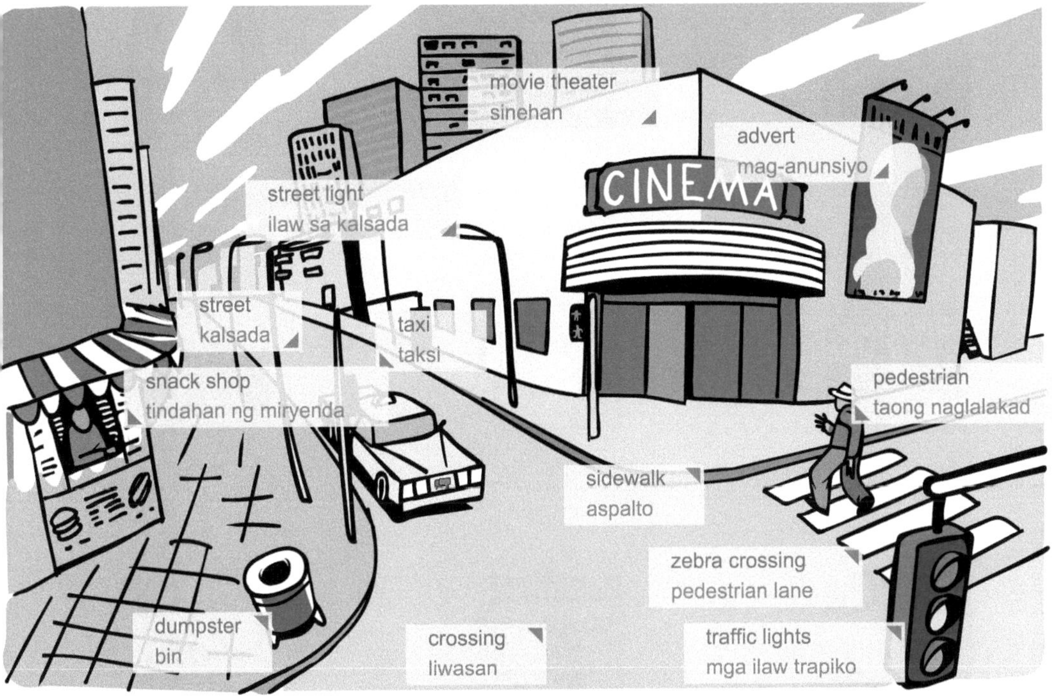

movie theater
sinehan

advert
mag-anunsiyo

street light
ilaw sa kalsada

CINEMA

street
kalsada

taxi
taksi

snack shop
tindahan ng miryenda

pedestrian
taong naglalakad

sidewalk
aspalto

zebra crossing
pedestrian lane

dumpster
bin

crossing
liwasan

traffic lights
mga ilaw trapiko

hut
kubo

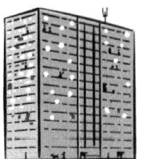

apartment
patag

train station
estasyon ng tren

city hall
munisipyo

museum
museo

school
paaralan

university

unibersidad

bank

bangko

hospital

ospital

hotel

hotel

pharmacy

parmasya

office

opisina

book shop

tindahan ng aklat

shop

tindahan

flower shop

tindahan ng bulaklak

supermarket

supermarket

market

palengke

department store

department store

fishmonger's shop

tindahan ng isda

mall

sentrong pamilihan

harbor

daungan

park

parke

bench

bangko

bridge

tulay

stairs

hagdan

subway

underground

tunnel

tunel

bus stop

hintuan ng bus

bar

bar

restaurant

restawran

postbox

kahon ng koreo

street sign

karatula sa kalsada

parking meter

metro ng paradahan

zoo

zoo

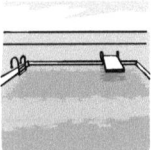

swimming pool

swimming pool

mosque

moske

farm

bukid

pollution

polusyon

cemetery

libingan

church

simbahan

playground

palaruan

temple

templo

landscape
tanawin

signpost
posteng pananda

path
daan

meadow
parang

stone
bato

tree
kahoy

hiker
hiker

river
ilog

grass
damo

flower
bulaklak

valley

lambak

hill

burol

lake

look

forest

kagubatan

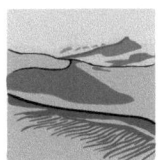

desert

disyerto

volcano

bulkan

castle

kastilyo

rainbow

bahaghari

mushroom

kabute

palm tree

palmera

mosquito

lamok

fly

langaw

ant

langgam

bee

bubuyog

spider

gagamba

beetle

salagubang

frog

palaka

squirrel

ardilya

hedgehog

parkupino

hare

liyebre

owl

kuwago

bird

ibon

swan

sisne

boar

bulugan

deer

usa

moose

moose

dam

dam

wind turbine

turbina ng hangin

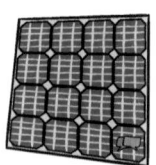

solar panel

solar panel

climate

klima

restaurant

restawran

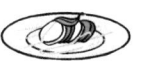

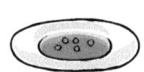

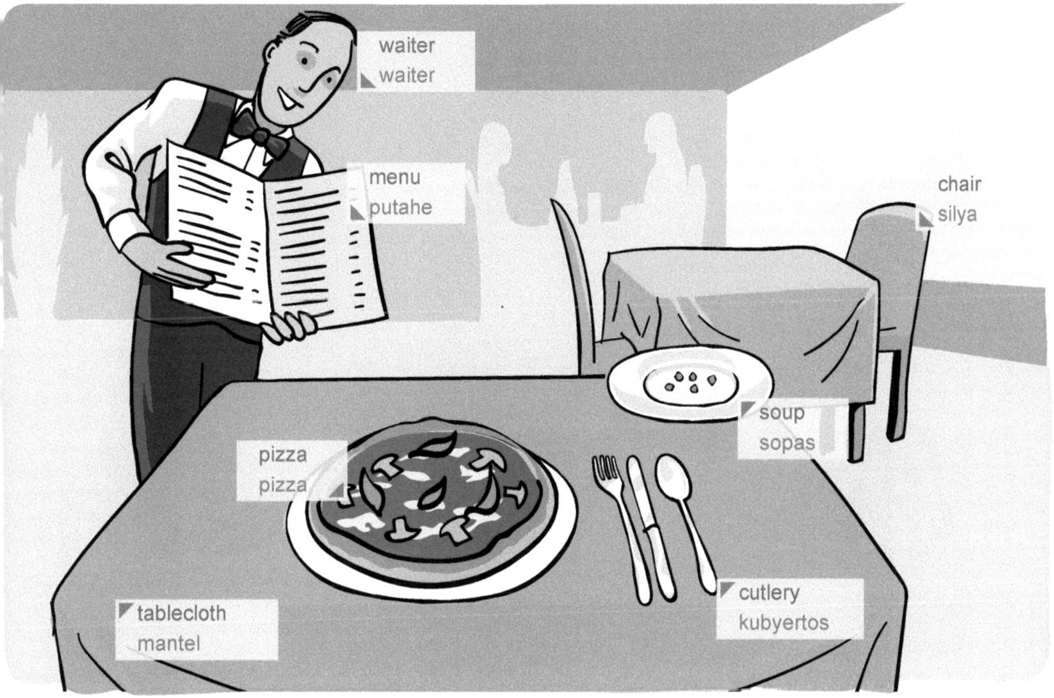
waiter
waiter
menu
putahe
chair
silya
soup
sopas
pizza
pizza
tablecloth
mantel
cutlery
kubyertos

starter
....
panimula

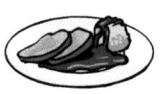

main course
....
pangunahing pagkain

dessert
....
panghimagas

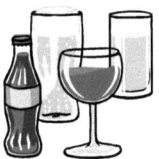

drinks
....
inumin

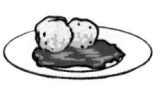

food
....
pagkain

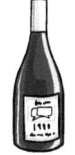

bottle
....
bote

fast food

fastfood

street food

pagkaing kalye

teapot

tsarera

sugar bowl

panutsa

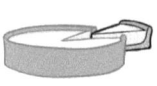

portion

bahagi

espresso machine

espresso machine

high chair

mataas na upuan

bill

bayarin

tray

bandehado

knife

kutsilyo

fork

tinidor

spoon

kutsara

teaspoon

kutsarita

serviette

serviette

glass

baso

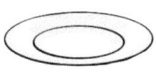

plate

pinggan

soup plate

platong pansopas

saucer

platito

sauce

sawsawan

salt shaker

pangkalog ng asin

pepper mill

panggiling ng paminta

vinegar

suka

oil

langis

spices

pampalasa

ketchup

ketsup

mustard

mustasa

mayonnaise

mayonnaise

special offer
espesyal na alok

customer
kustomer

dairy products
produktong mantikilya

FOR

fruit
prutas

shopping cart
troli

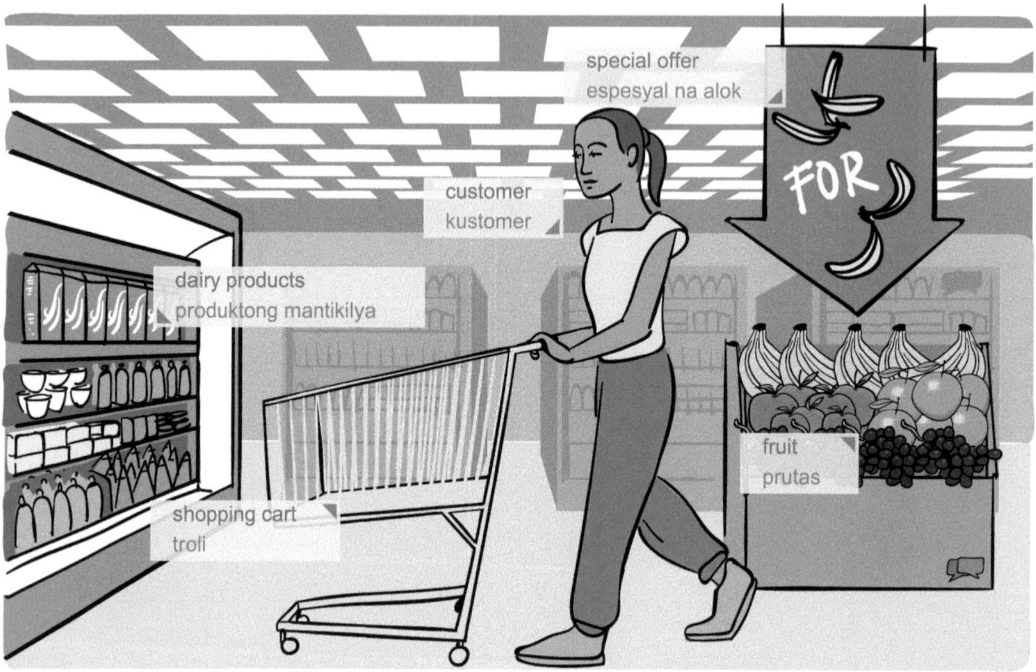

butcher's shop
butser

bakery
panaderya

weigh
timbang

vegetables
mga gulay

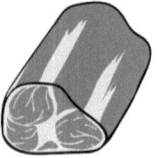

meat
karne

frozen food
pinalamig na pagkain

cold cuts

malamig na karne

canned food

delatang pagkain

detergent

pulbos na panlaba

candy

matatamis

household products

mga produktong pambahay

cleaning products

mga produktong panlinis

sales representative

tindera

cash register

cash register

cashier

kahera

shopping list

listahan ng pinamili

opening hours

oras ng pagbubukas

wallet

pitaka

credit card

credit card

bag

bag

plastic bag

plastik bag

water

tubig

juice

juice

milk

gatas

coke

coke

wine

alak

beer

serbesa

alcohol

alak

cocoa

kakaw

tea

tsaa

coffee

kape

espresso

espresso

cappuccino

cappuccino

banana

saging

apple

mansanas

orange

kahel

melon

melon

lemon

limon

carrot

carrot

garlic

bawang

bamboo

kawayan

onion

sibuyas

mushroom

kabute

nuts

mani

noodles

noodles

spaghetti

spaghetti

rice

bigas

salad

ensalada

fries

chips

fried potatoes

pritong patatas

pizza

pizza

hamburger

hamburger

sandwich

sandwich

escalope

piraso ng karneng walang buto

ham

hamon

salami

salami

sausage

tsoriso

chicken

manok

roast

inihaw

fish

isda

food - pagkain

porridge oats

mga porridge oat

muesli

muesli

cornflakes

cornflakes

flour

harina

croissant

croissant

bread roll

rolyong tinapay

bread

tinapay

toast

tostado

cookies

biskuwit

butter

mantikilya

curd

keso

cake

keyk

egg

itlog

fried egg

pritong itlog

cheese

keso

ice cream

sorbetes

sugar

asukal

honey

pulot

jelly

jam

nougat cream

tsokolateng pinapahid

curry

curry

goat	cow	calf
kambing	baka	guya

pig	piglet	bull
baboy	biik	toro

goose

gansa

duck

pato

chick

sisiw

hen

inahin

cockerel

katyaw

rat

daga

cat

pusa

mouse

daga

ox

kapong baka

dog

aso

dog house

bahay ng aso

garden hose

hose sa hardin

watering can

latang pandilig

scythe

haras

plow

araro

sickle

karit

hoe

asarol

pitchfork

tuhugin

axe

palakol

pushcart

karitela

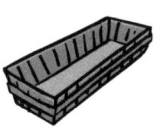

trough

sabsaban

milk can

lata ng gatas

sack

sako

fence

bakod

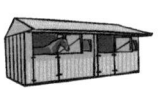

stable

kuwadra

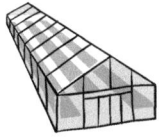

greenhouse

punlaan

soil

lupa

seed

buto

fertilizer

pataba

combine harvester

combine harvester

harvest

mag-ani

harvest

ani

yams

yams

wheat

trigo

soya

soya

potato

patatas

corn

mais

rapeseed

rapeseed

fruit tree

kahoy na namumunga

manioc

kamoteng kahoy

grain

siryal

house
bahay

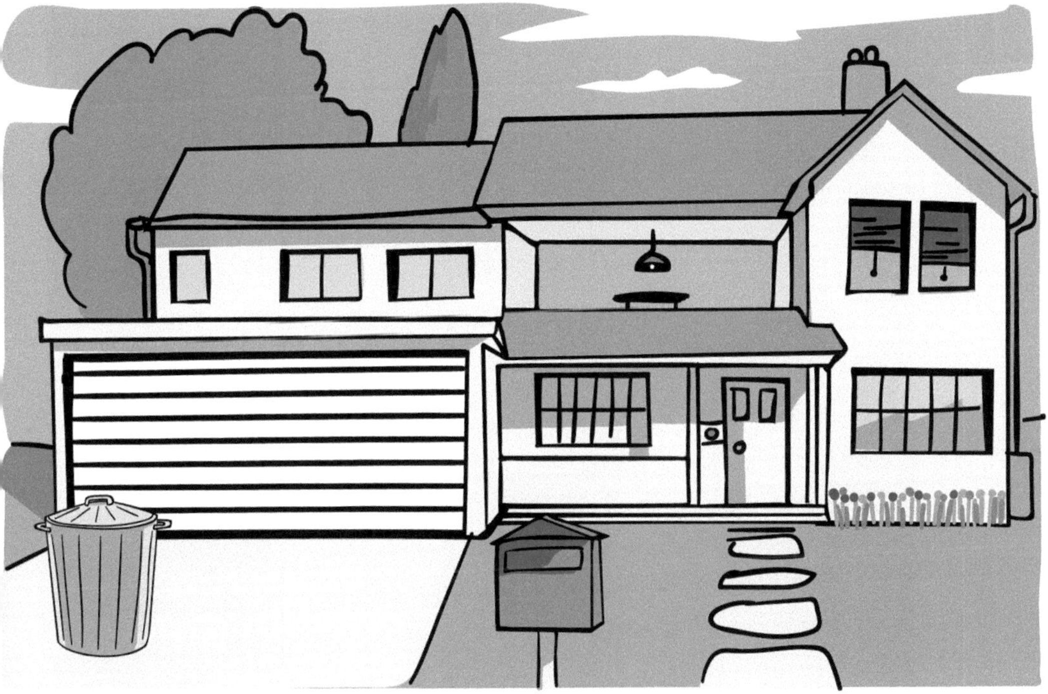

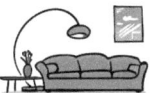

living room
salas

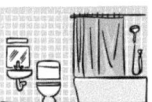

bathroom
palikuran

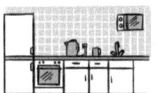

kitchen
kusina

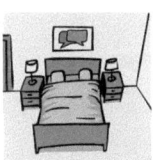

bedroom
silid-tulugan

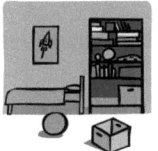

kids room
silid ng bata

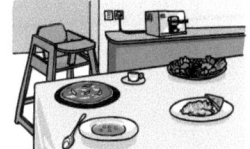

dining room
hapag-kainan

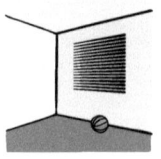

floor

sahig

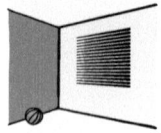

wall

pader

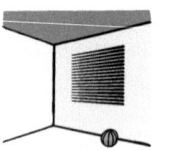

ceiling

kisame

cellar

bodega ng alak

sauna

sauna

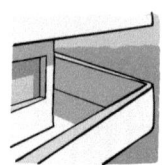

balcony

balkonahe

terrace

terasa

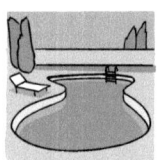

pool

pool

lawn mower

pamputol ng damo

sheet

piraso ng papel

bedspread

kobrekama

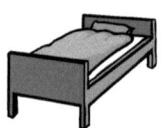

bed

higaan

broom

walis

bucket

timba

switch

pindutan

carpet

karpet

drape

kurtina

table

mesa

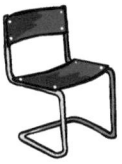

chair

silya

rocking chair

tumba-tumba

armchair

sandalan

book

aklat

blanket

kumot

decoration

dekorasyon

firewood

kahoy na panggatong

film

pelikula

stereo system

hi-fi

key

susi

newspaper

dyaryo

painting

pinta

poster

poster

radio

radyo

notebook

kuwaderno

vacuum cleaner

vacuum cleaner

cactus

kaktus

candle

kandila

kitchen
kusina

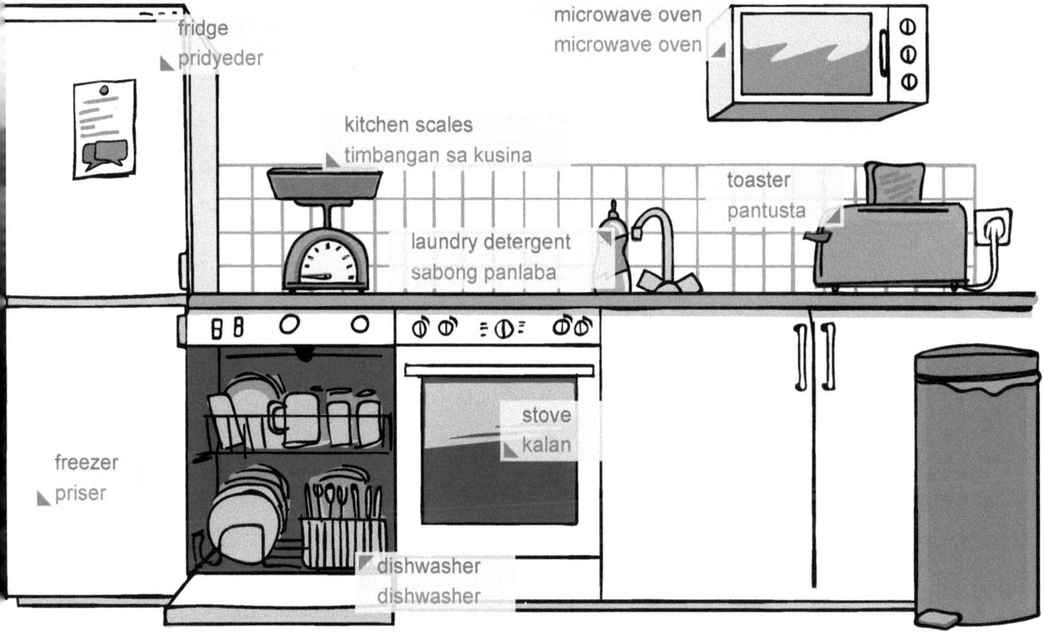
fridge
pridyeder
microwave oven
microwave oven
kitchen scales
timbangan sa kusina
toaster
pantusta
laundry detergent
sabong panlaba
stove
kalan
freezer
priser
dishwasher
dishwasher

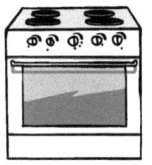

cooker

lutuan

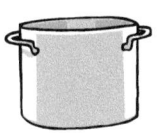

pot

kaldero

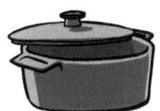

cast-iron pot

kalderong bakal

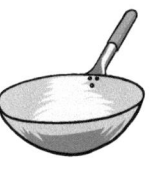

wok / kadai

wok / kadai

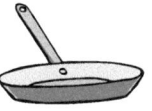

pan

kawali

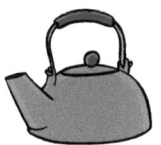

kettle

takore

steamer

pasingawan

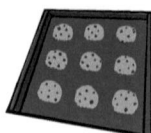

baking tray

bandehado sa paghuhurno

crockery

babasagin

mug

mug

bowl

mangkok

chopsticks

sipit ng intsik

ladle

sandok

spatula

spatula

whisk

pampalis

strainer

pansala

sieve

salaan

grater

pangkayod

mortar

almires

barbecue

barbikyo

fireplace

siga

chopping board

tadtaran

rolling pin

rodilyo

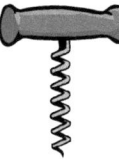

corkscrew

tribuson

can

lata

can opener

pambukas ng lata

oven cloth

panghawak ng kaldero

sink

lababo

brush

bras

sponge

espongha

blender

blender

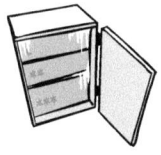

deep freezer

malalim na freezer

baby bottle

bote ng sanggol

tap

gripo

bathroom
palikuran

heating
pampainit
towel
tuwalya
shower
shower
shower curtain
kurtina sa shower
bubble bath
bubble bath
bathtub
banyera
glass
baso
washing machine
washing machine
tap
gripo
tiles
tiles
potty
arinola
sink
lababo

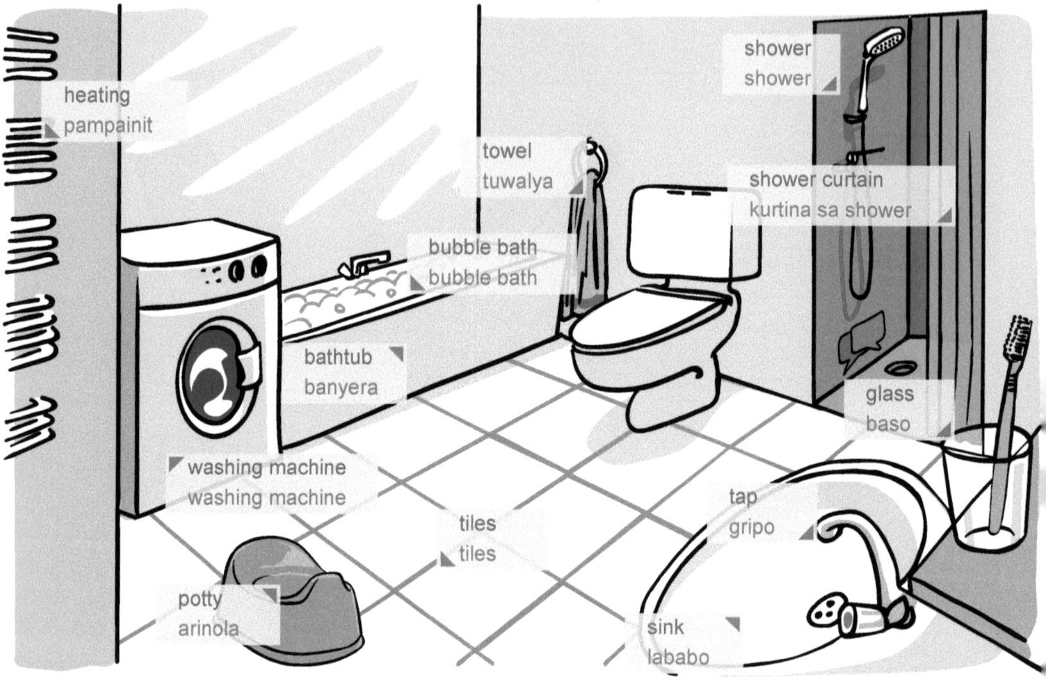

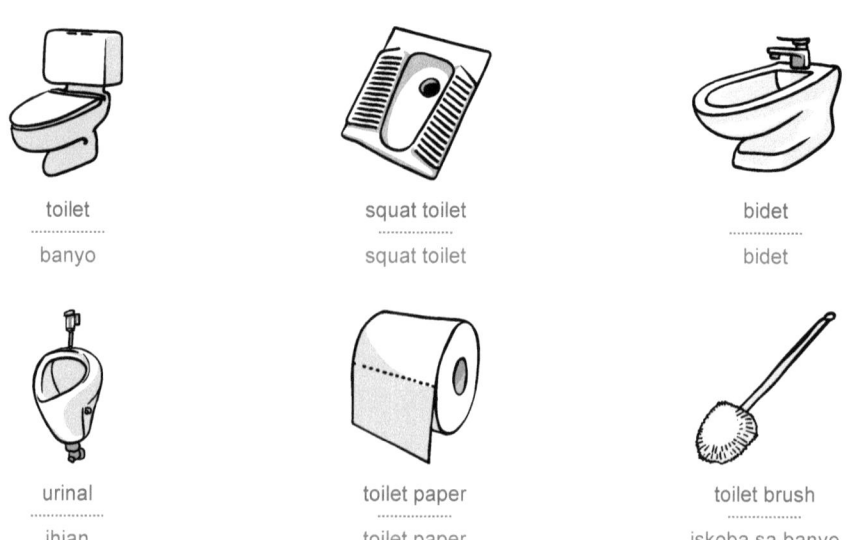

toilet

banyo

squat toilet

squat toilet

bidet

bidet

urinal

ihian

toilet paper

toilet paper

toilet brush

iskoba sa banyo

toothbrush

sipilyo

toothpaste

tutpeyst

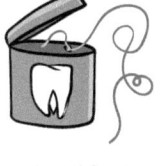

dental floss

dental floss

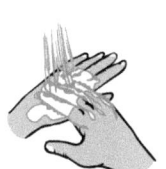

wash

hugasan

hand shower

shower na hinahawakan

douche

dutsa

basin

palanggana

back brush

bras panlikod

soap

sabon

shower gel

shower gel

shampoo

shampoo

flannel

pranela

drain

paagusan

creme

krema

deodorant

deodorant

mirror

salamin

hand mirror

salaming hinahawakan

razor

pang-ahit

shaving foam

bulang pang-ahit

aftershave

aftershave

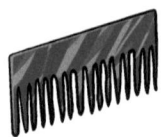

comb

suklay

brush

brush

hair-dryer

pantuyo ng buhok

hairspray

sprey sa buhok

makeup

makeup

lipstick

lipistik

nail varnish

pampakintab ng kuko

cotton wool

bulak na lana

nail scissors

panggupit ng kuko

perfume

pabango

washbag

washbag

stool

stool

weighing scales

timbangan

bathrobe

bata

rubber gloves

gomang guwantes

tampon

tampon

sanitary towel

malinis na tuwalya

chemical toilet

chemical toilet

kids room

silid ng bata

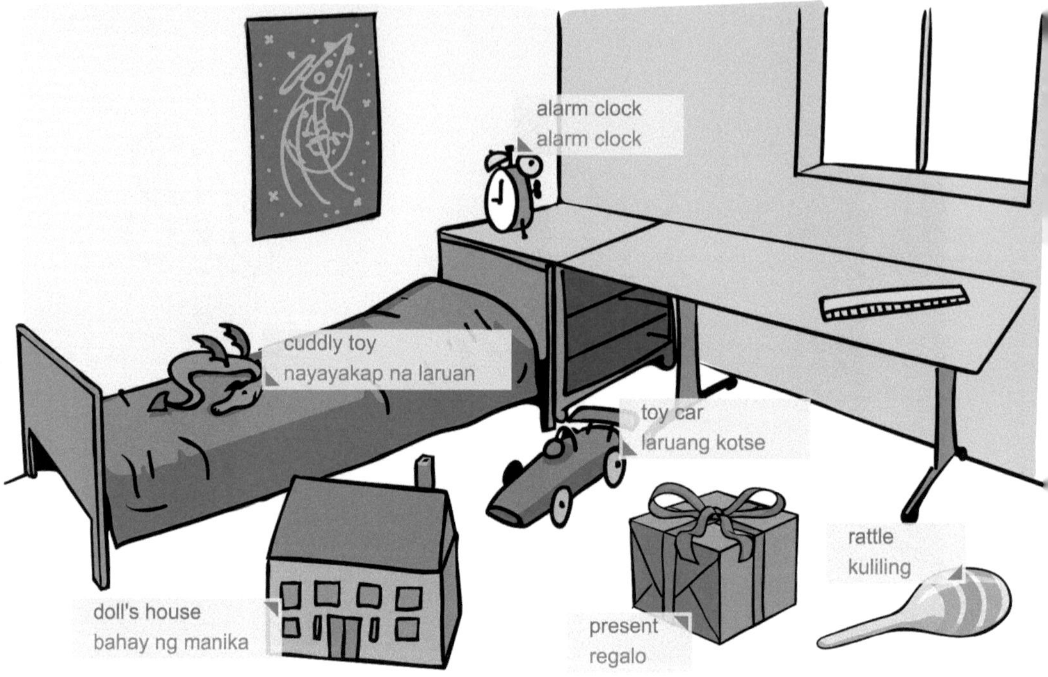

alarm clock
alarm clock
cuddly toy
nayayakap na laruan
toy car
laruang kotse
rattle
kuliling
doll's house
bahay ng manika
present
regalo

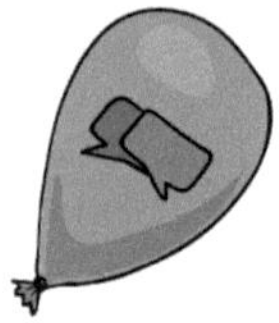

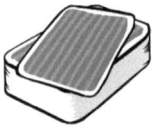

balloon
lobo

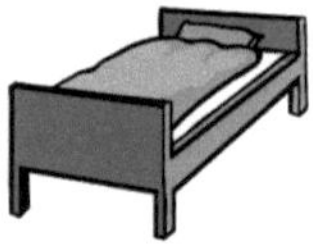

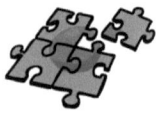

bed
higaan

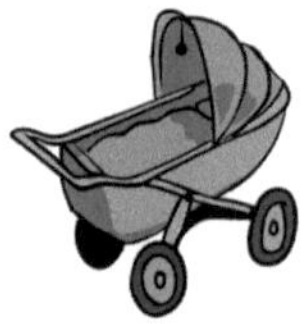

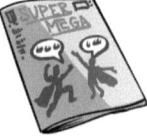

stroller
pram

deck of cards
hanay ng mga baraha

jigsaw
jigsaw

SUPER
MEGA

comic
komiks

lego bricks

lego bricks

toy blocks

blokeng laruan

action figure

action figure

romper suit

paglaki ng sanggol

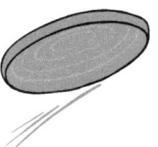

frisbee

frisbee

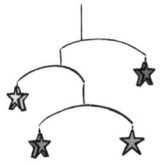

mobile

mobile

board game

board game

dice

dice

model train set

model train set

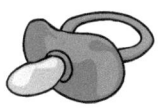

pacifier

manikin

party

salu-salo

picture book

aklat ng mga litrato

ball

bola

doll

manika

play

maglaro

sandpit

tibagan ng buhangin

swing

duyan

toys

mga laruan

video game console

video game console

tricycle

traysikel

teddy bear

teddy bear

wardrobe

aparador

clothing

pananamit

socks

medyas

stockings

stockings

tights

pampitis

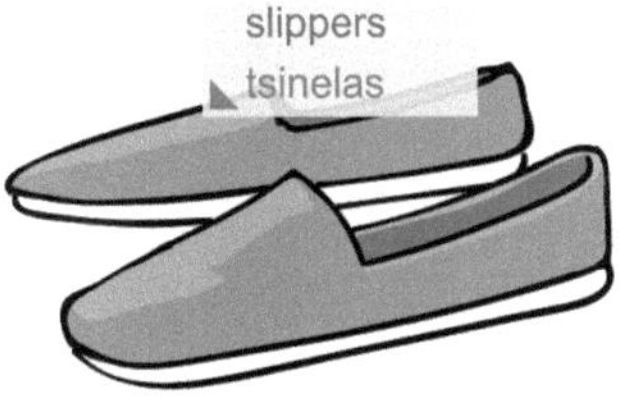

scarf
bandana

umbrella
payong

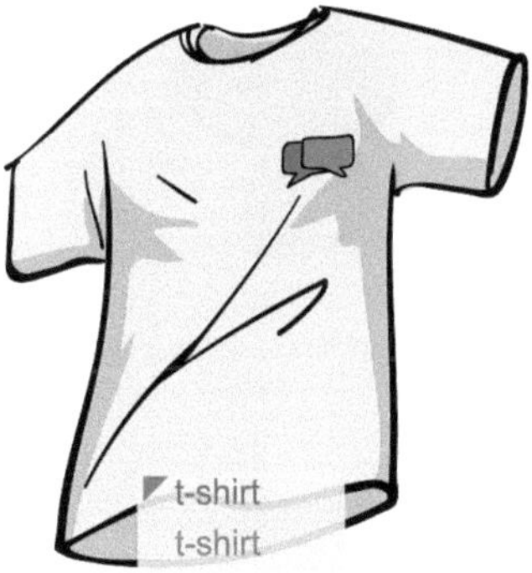

t-shirt
t-shirt

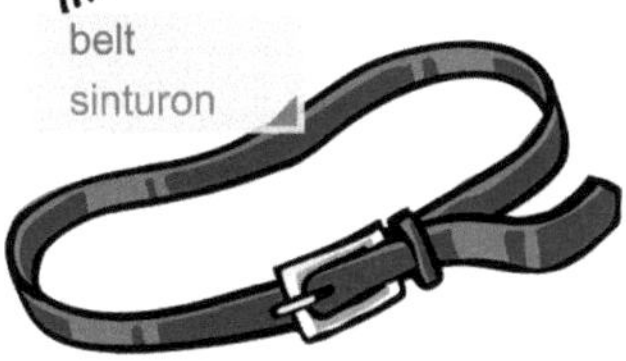

belt
sinturon

boots
bota

slippers
tsinelas

sneakers
sneakers

sandals
....
sandalyas

shoes
....
sapatos

rubber boots
....
botang degoma

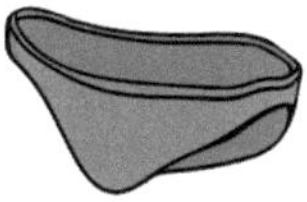

underwear
....
salawal

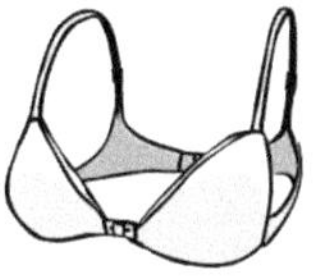

bra
....
bra

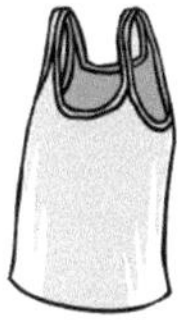

undershirt
....
tsaleko

body

katawan

pants

pantalon

jeans

jeans

skirt

palda

blouse

blusa

shirt

kamiseta

pullover

pullover

sweater

panlamig

blazer

blazer

jacket

diyaket

coat

kapa

raincoat

kapote

costume

kasuotan

dress

bistida

wedding dress

damit pangkasal

suit

terno

nightgown

damit pantulog

pajamas

padyama

sari

sari

headscarf

bandana sa ulo

turban

turban

burka

burka

kaftan

kaftan

abaya

abaya

swimsuit

panlangoy

trunks

trunks

shorts

salawal

tracksuit

tracksuit

apron

apron

gloves

guwantes

button

butones

glasses

salamin

bracelet

pulseras

necklace

kuwintas

ring

singsing

earring

hikaw

cap

takip

coat hanger

sabitan ng kapa

hat

sombrero

tie

kurbata

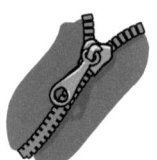

zip

siper

helmet

helmet

braces

tirante

school uniform

uniporme sa paaralan

uniform

uniporme

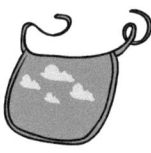

bib

bibero

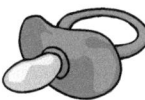

pacifier

manikin

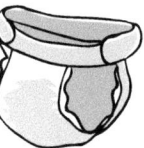

diaper

lampin

office

opisina

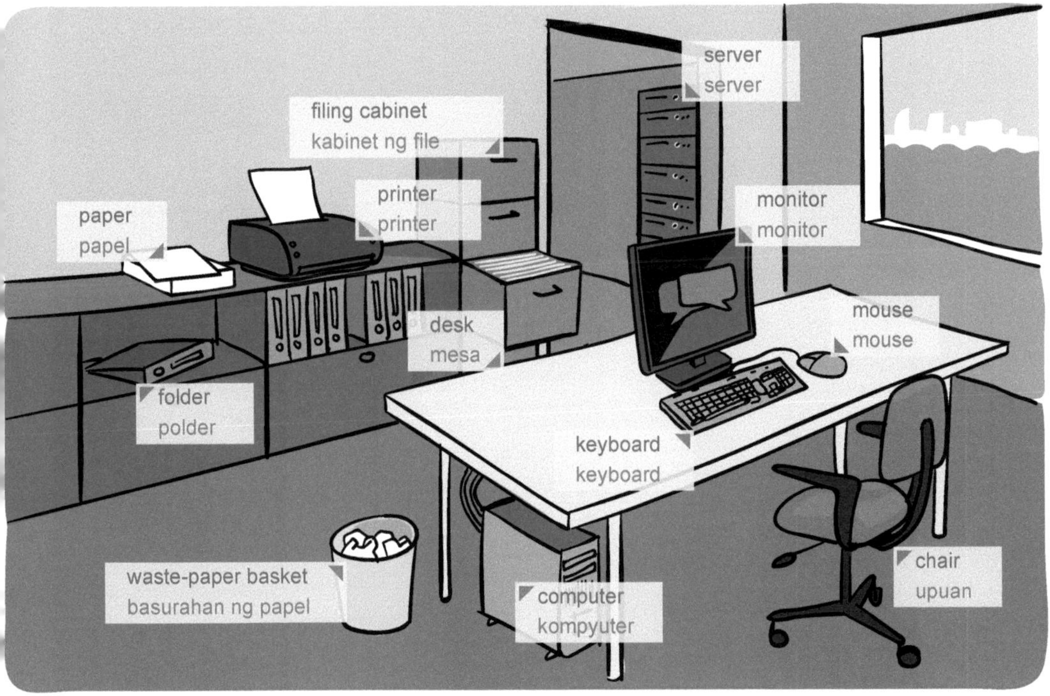

server
server
filing cabinet
kabinet ng file
printer
printer
paper
papel
monitor
monitor
mouse
mouse
desk
mesa
folder
polder
keyboard
keyboard
waste-paper basket
basurahan ng papel
chair
upuan
computer
kompyuter

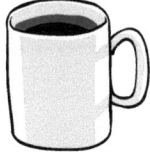

coffee mug

tasa ng kape

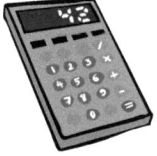

calculator

calculator

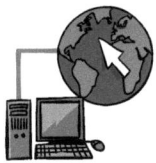

internet

internet

laptop

laptop

letter

sulat

message

mensahe

cell phone

mobile

network

network

photocopier

photocopier

software

software

telephone

telepono

plug socket

saksakan

fax machine

fax machine

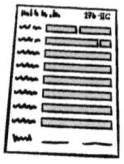

form

anyo

document

dokumento

buy

bumili

pay

magbayad

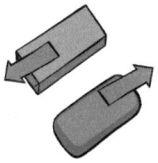

trade

ikalakal

money

pera

dollar

dolyar

euro

euro

yen

yen

rouble

rublo

Swiss franc

swiss franc

renminbi yuan

renminbi yuan

rupee

rupee

cash point

cash point

currency exchange office

tanggapan ng palitan ng pera

gold

ginto

silver

tanso

oil

langis

energy

enerhiya

price

presyo

contract

kontrata

tax

buwis

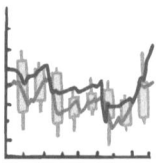

stock

stock

work

trabaho

employee

empleyado

employer

taga-empleyo

factory

pabrika

shop

tindahan

occupations
mga trabaho

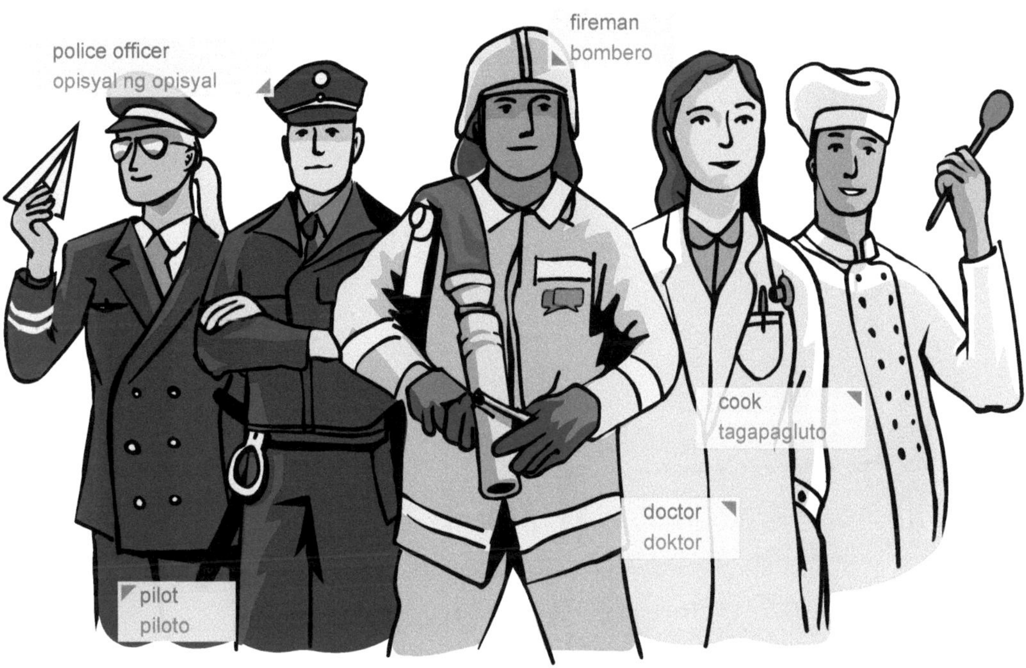
police officer
opisyal ng opisyal
fireman
bombero
cook
tagapagluto
doctor
doktor
pilot
piloto

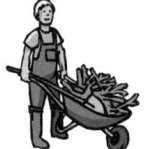

gardener

hardinero

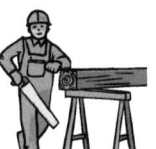

carpenter

karpentero

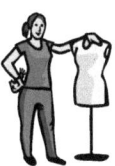

seamstress

mananahi

judge

hukom

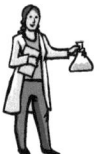

chemist

kemiko

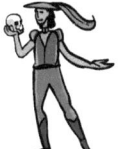

actor

aktor

bus driver

tsuper ng bus

taxi driver

tsuper ng taxi

fisherman

mangingisda

cleaning lady

tagapaglinis

roofer

tagapagkabit ng bubong

waiter

waiter

hunter

mangangaso

painter

pintor

baker

panadero

electrician

elektrisyan

builder

tagapagtayo

engineer

inhinyero

butcher

magkakarne

plumber

tubero

postman

kartero

soldier

sundalo

architect

arkitekto

cashier

kahera

florist

magtitinda ng bulaklak

hairdresser

manggugupit

conductor

konduktor

mechanic

mekaniko

captain

kapitan

dentist

dentista

scientist

siyentipiko

rabbi

rabbi

imam

imam

monk

monghe

pastor

klero

tools

mga kagamitan

hammer
martilyo
pliers
plais
screwdriver
distornilyador
wrench
lyabe
torch
tanglaw

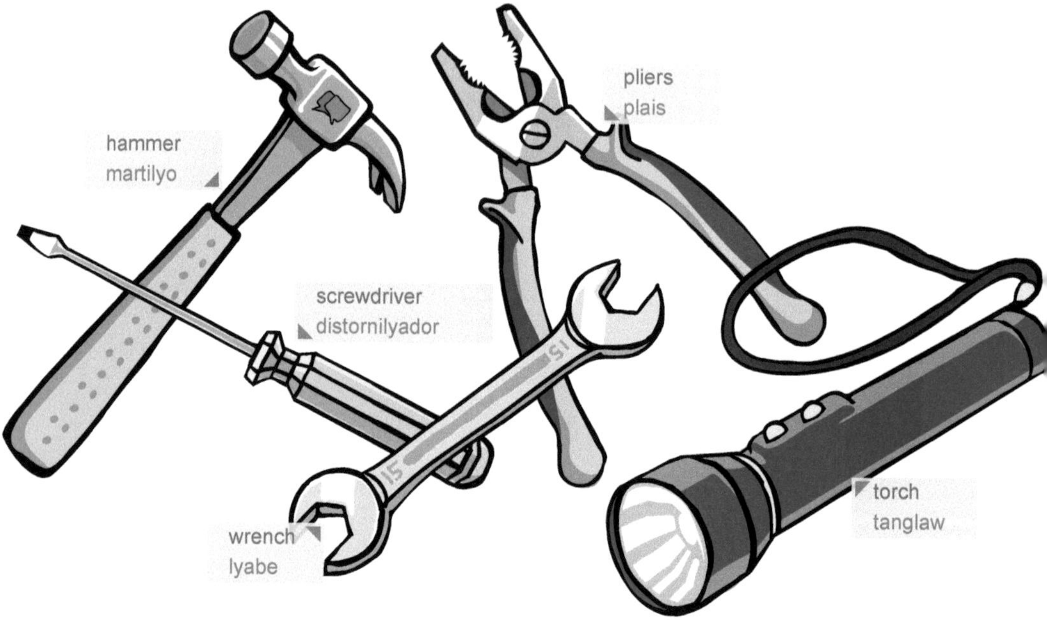

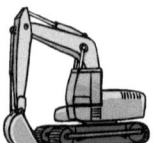

excavator

panghukay

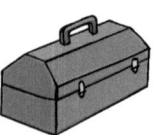

toolbox

toolbox

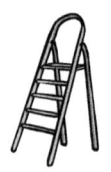

ladder

hagdan

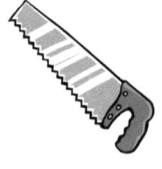

saw

lagari

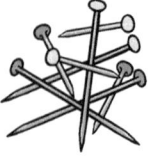

nails

mga pako

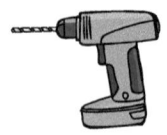

drill

pambutas

repair

kumpunihin

shovel

pala

Damn!

Kainis!

dustpan

pandakot

paint can

palayok ng pintura

screws

mga tornilyo

musical instruments
mga pangmusikang instrumento

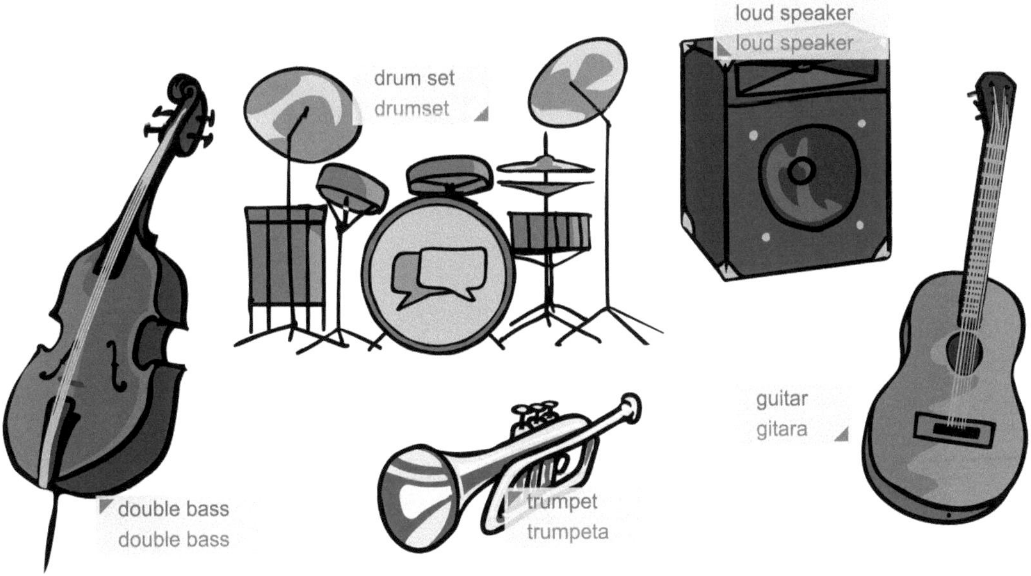

drum set
drumset

loud speaker
loud speaker

guitar
gitara

double bass
double bass

trumpet
trumpeta

piano

piyano

violin

biyolin

bass

bass

timpani

timpani

drums

mga drum

keyboard

keyboard

saxophone

saksopon

flute

plauta

microphone

mikropono

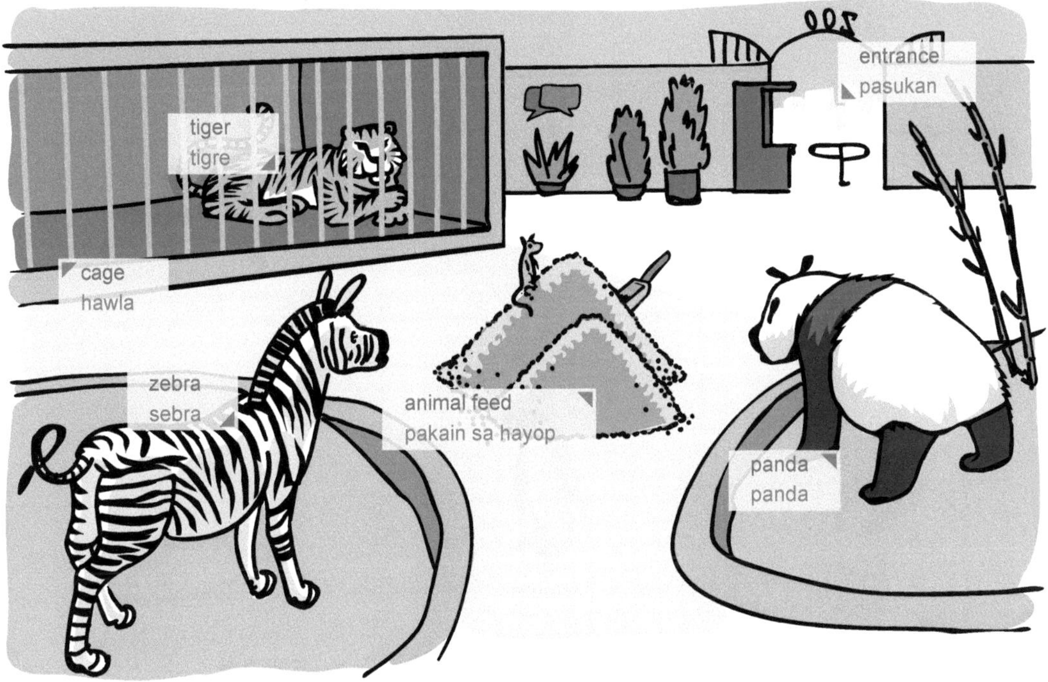

entrance
pasukan

tiger
tigre

cage
hawla

zebra
sebra

animal feed
pakain sa hayop

panda
panda

animals

mga hayop

elephant

elepante

kangaroo

kanggaro

rhino

rhino

gorilla

gorilya

bear

oso

camel

kamelyo

ostrich

ostrich

lion

leon

monkey

unggoy

flamingo

flamingo

parrot

loro

polar bear

polar bear

penguin

penguin

shark

pating

peacock

paboreal

snake

ahas

crocodile

buwaya

zookeeper

tagapag-alaga ng zoo

seal

seal

jaguar

jaguar

pony
buriko

leopard
leopardo

hippo
hipo

giraffe
dyirap

eagle
agila

boar
bulugan

fish
isda

turtle
pagong

walrus
walrus

fox
soro

gazelle
gasel

American football
Amerikanong putbol

cycling
pamimisikleta

tennis
tennis

basketball
basketbol

swimming
paglalangoy

boxing
boksing

ice hockey
ice-hockey

soccer
soccer

badminton
badminton

athletics
atletiks

handball
handball

skiing
skiing

polo
polo

activities
mga aktibidad

laugh
tumawa
jump
tumalon
hug
yakapin
walk
lumakad
sing
kumanta
dream
mangarap
pray
magdasal
kiss
halikan

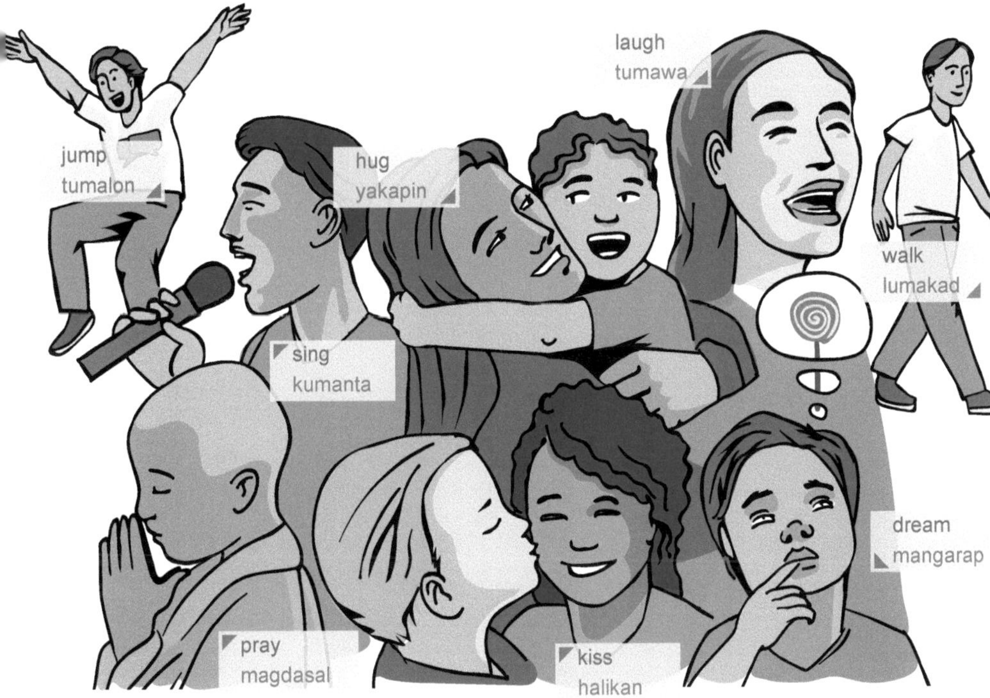

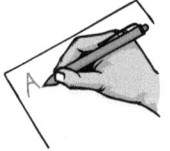

write

sumulat

draw

gumuhit

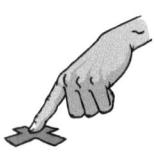

show

ipakita

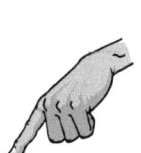

push

itulak

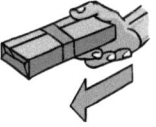

give

magbigay

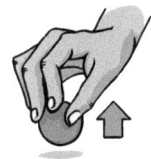

take

kunin

have

magkaroon

do

gawin

be

maging

stand

tumayo

run

tumakbo

pull

hilahin

throw

itapon

fall

malaglag

lie

mahiga

wait

hintayin

carry

dalhin

sit

umupo

get dressed

magbihis

sleep

matulog

wake up

gumising

look at

tumingin

cry

umiyak

stroke

estilo

comb

magsuklay

talk

magsalita

understand

intindihin

ask

magtanong

listen

makinig

drink

uminom

eat

kumain

tidy up

linisin

love

mahal

cook

magluto

drive

magmaneho

fly

lumipad

sail

maglayag

calculate

kalkulahin

read

basahin

learn

matuto

work

trabaho

marry

pakasalan

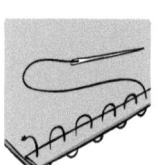

sew

tahiin

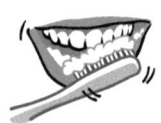

brush teeth

magsipilyo ng ngipin

kill

patayin

smoke

manigarilyo

send

magpadala

grandmother
lola

grandfather
lolo

father
ama

mother
ina

baby
sanggol

daughter
anak na babae

son
anak na lalaki

guest

panauhin

aunt

tiya

uncle

tiyo

brother

kuya

sister

ate

body

katawan

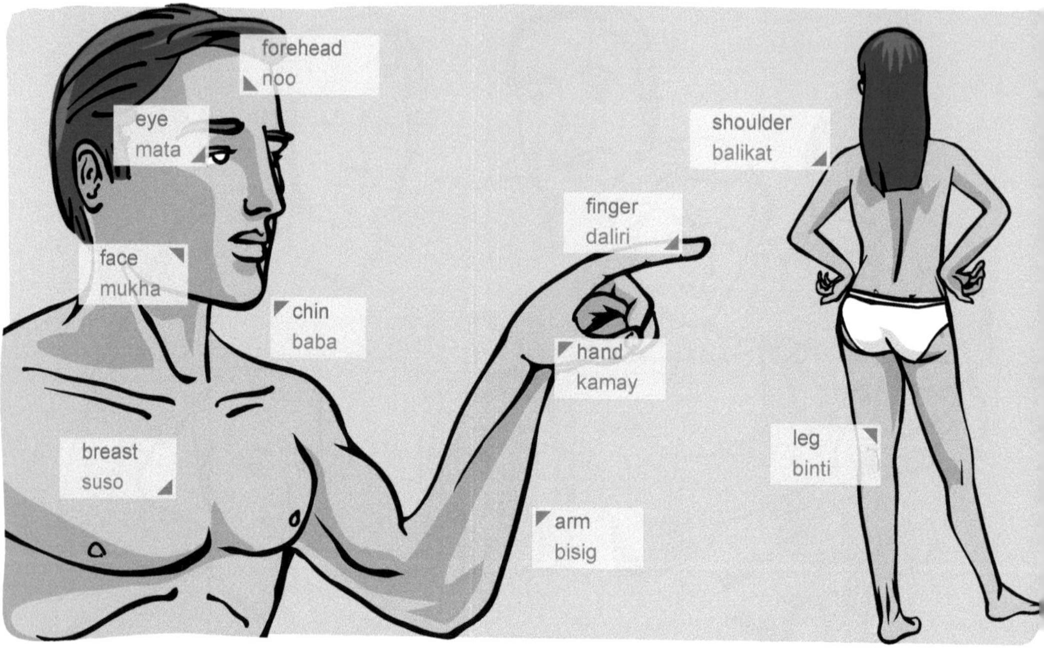

forehead
noo

eye
mata

shoulder
balikat

finger
daliri

face
mukha

chin
baba

hand
kamay

breast
suso

leg
binti

arm
bisig

baby
sanggol

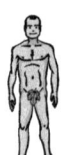

man
lalaki

woman
babae

girl
batang babae

boy
batang lalaki

head
ulo

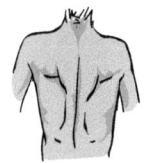

back

likod

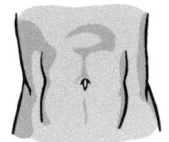

belly

tiyan

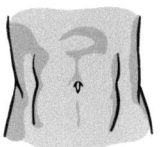

navel

pusod

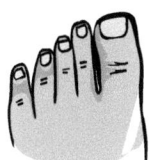

toe

daliri ng paa

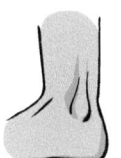

heel

takong

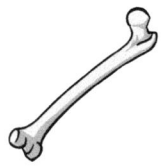

bone

buto

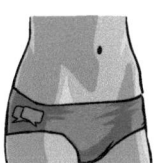

hip

balakang

knee

tuhod

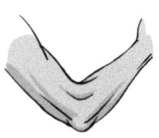

elbow

siko

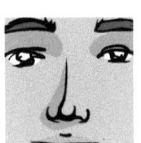

nose

ilong

buttocks

gitna

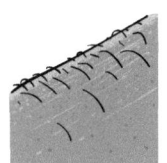

skin

balat

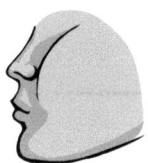

cheek

pisngi

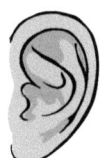

ear

tainga

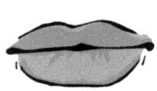

lip

labi

mouth

bibig

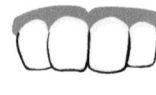

tooth

ngipin

tongue

dila

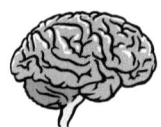

brain

utak

heart

puso

muscle

kalamnan

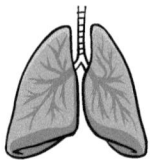

lung

baga

liver

atay

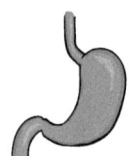

stomach

sikmura

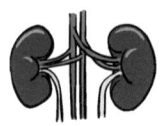

kidneys

mga bato

sex

pagtatalik

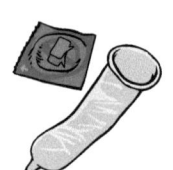

condom

kondom

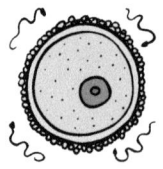

ovum

obyum

semen

semen

pregnancy

pagbubuntis

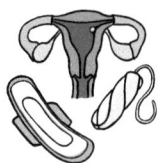

menstruation
....
pagreregla

vagina
....
vagina

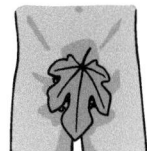

penis
....
ari ng lalaki

eyebrow
....
kilay

hair
....
buhok

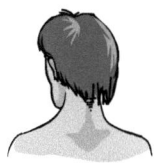

neck
....
leeg

hospital
ospital

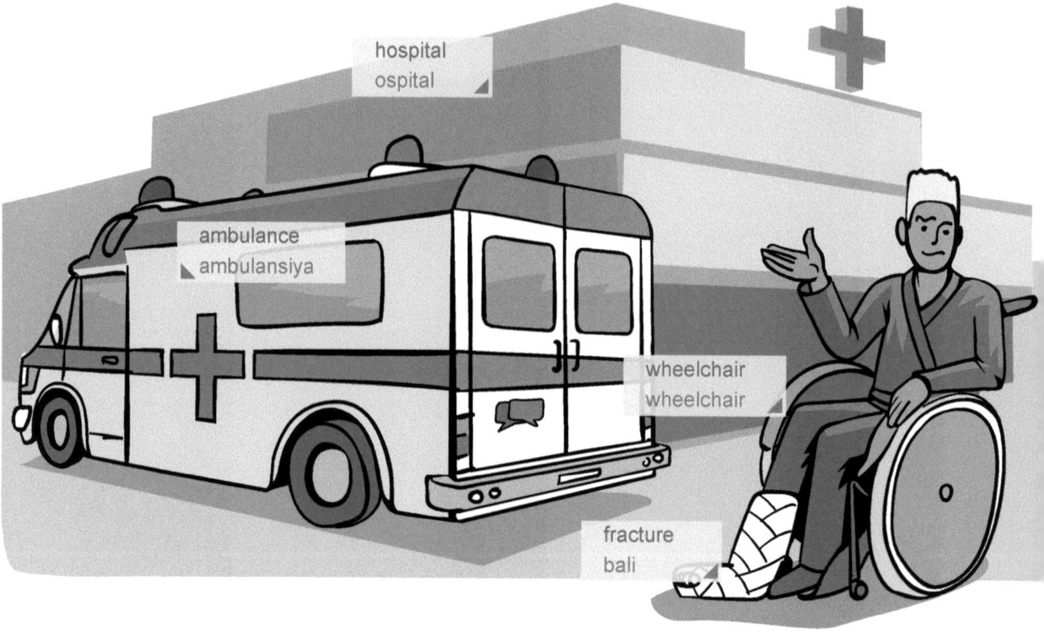

hospital
ospital
ambulance
ambulansiya
wheelchair
wheelchair
fracture
bali

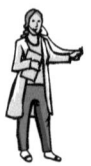

doctor
doktor

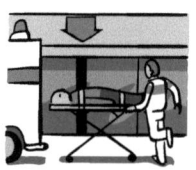

emergency room
silid pang-emergency

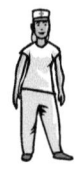

nurse
nars

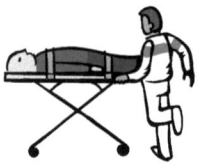

emergency
emerhensiya

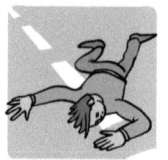

unconscious
walang malay

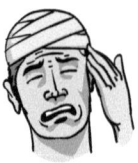

pain
pananakit

injury

pinsala

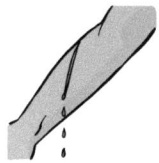

bleeding

nagdurugo

heart attack

atake sa puso

stroke

atake serebral

allergy

alerdye

cough

ubo

fever

lagnat

flu

trangkaso

diarrhea

pagdudumi

headache

sakit ng ulo

cancer

kanser

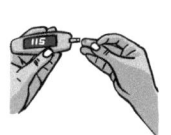

diabetes

diyabetis

surgeon

siruhano

scalpel

iskalpel

operation

operasyon

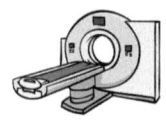

CT

CT

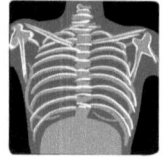

x-ray

x-ray

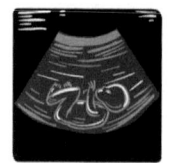

ultrasound

ultrasound

face mask

maskara sa mukha

disease

sakit

waiting room

silid-antayan

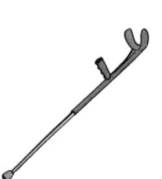

crutch

saklay

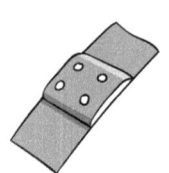

plaster

plaster

bandage

benda

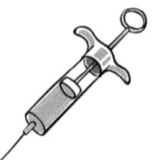

injection

iniksyon

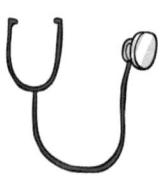

stethoscope

istetoskopyo

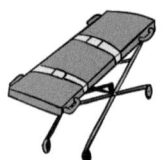

stretcher

estretser

clinical thermometer

klinikal na termometro

birth

pagsilang

overweight

labis sa timbang

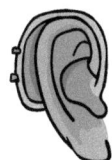

hearing aid

hearing-aid

disinfectant

pang-disimpekta

infection

impeksyon

virus

bayrus

HIV / AIDS

HIV / AIDS

medicine

medisina

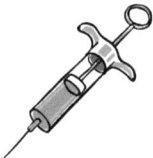

vaccination

bakuna

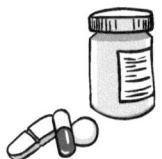

tablets

mga tableta

pill

tabletas

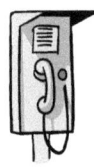

emergency call

emergency na tawag

blood pressure monitor

pagmamatyag sa presyon
ng dugo

ill / healthy

may sakit / malusog

Help!

Tulong!

alarm

alarma

assault

asulto

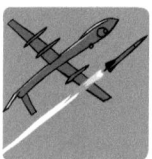

attack

atake

danger

panganib

emergency exit

labasang pang-emergency

Fire!

Sunog!

fire extinguisher

fire extinguisher

accident

aksidente

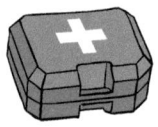

first-aid kit

kagamitan sa paunang
lunas

SOS

SOS

police

pulis

Europe

Europa

North America

Hilagang Amerika

South America

Timog Amerika

Africa

Aprika

Asia

Asya

Australia

Australia

Atlantic

Atlantika

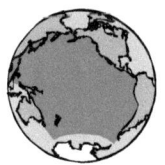

Pacific

Pasipiko

Indian Ocean

Dagat Indiano

Antarctic Ocean

Dagat Antarktika

Arctic Ocean

Dapat Arktika

North pole

Hilagang polo

South pole

Timog polo

Antarctica

Antartika

earth

mundo

land

lupa

sea

dagat

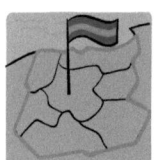

island

isla

nation

bansa

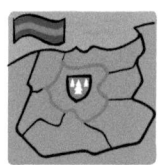

state

estado

clock face

mukha ng orasan

hour hand

orasang kamay

minute hand

minutong kamay

second hand

segundong kamay

What time is it?

Anong oras na?

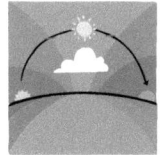

day

araw

time

oras

now

ngayon

digital watch

digital na relo

minute

minuto

hour

oras

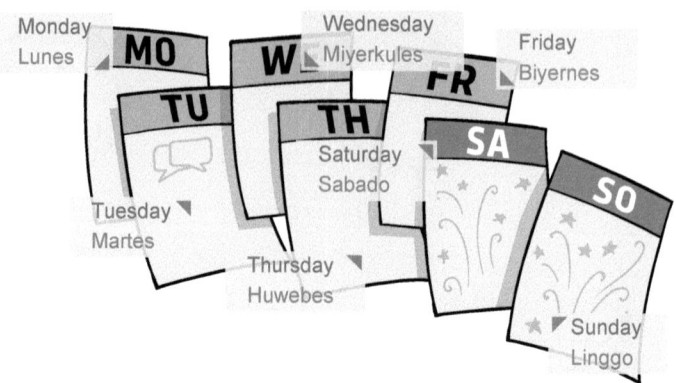

Monday / Lunes — MO
Tuesday / Martes — TU
Wednesday / Miyerkules — W
Thursday / Huwebes — TH
Friday / Biyernes — FR
Saturday / Sabado — SA
Sunday / Linggo — SO

yesterday
kahapon

today
ngayon

tomorrow
bukas

morning
umaga

noon
tanghali

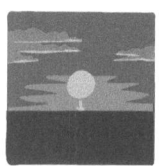

evening
gabi

workdays
mga araw ng negosyo

weekend
katapusan ng linggo

year

taon

rain
ulan
spring
tagsibol
summer
tag-init
wind
hangin
fall
taglagas
snow
niyebe
winter
taglamig

4.APRIL 11°
5.APRIL 4°
6.APRIL 13°
7.APRIL 8°
8.APRIL 10°

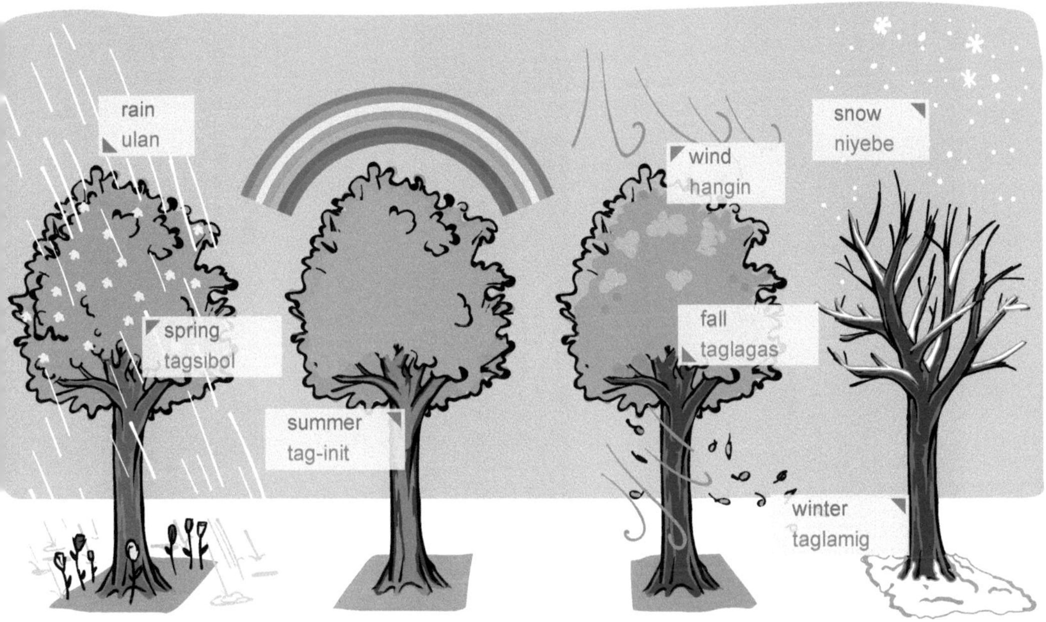

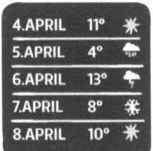

weather forecast

lagay ng panahon

F
C
120
90
60
30
0
-30
40
30
20
10
0
-10
-20

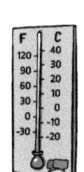

thermometer

termometro

sunshine

sikat ng araw

cloud

ulap

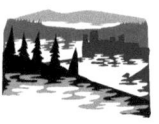

fog

hamog

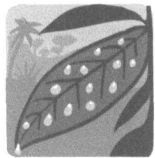

humidity

kahalumigmigan

lightning

kidlat

thunder

kulog

storm

bagyo

hail

may yelong ulan

monsoon

tag-ulan

flood

pagkain

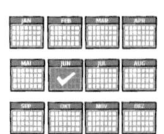

ice

yelo

January

Enero

February

Pebrero

March

Marso

April

Abril

May

Mayo

June

Hunyo

July

Hulyo

August

Agosto

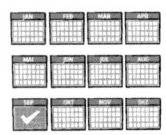

September
....
Setyembre

October
....
Oktubre

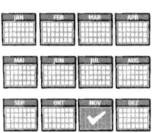

November
....
Nobyembre

December
....
Disyembre

shapes

mga hugis

circle
....
bilog

square
....
parisukat

rectangle
....
rektanggulo

triangle
....
tatsulok

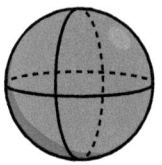

sphere
....
pabilog

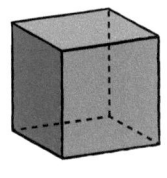

cube
....
kyub

white
....
puti

yellow
....
dilaw

orange
....
kahel

pink
....
rosas

red
....
pula

purple
....
ube

blue
....
asul

green
....
berde

brown
....
brown

gray
....
grey

black
....
itim

a lot / a little

marami / kakaunti

angry / calm

takot / kalmado

beautiful / ugly

maganda / pangit

beginning / end

simula / katapusan

big / small

malaki / maliit

bright / dark

matingkad / madilim

brother / sister

kuya / ate

clean / dirty

malinis / madumi

complete / incomplete

kumpleto / kulang

day / night

araw / gabi

dead / alive

patay / buhay

wide / narrow

malawak / makipot

edible / inedible

nakakain / hindi nakakain

evil / kind

masama / mabuti

excited / bored

nakakatuwa / nakakainip

fat / thin

mataba / payat

first / last

una / huli

friend / enemy

kaibigan / kaaway

full / empty

puno / walang laman

hard / soft

matigas / malambot

heavy / light

mabigat / magaan

hunger / thirst

gutom / uhaw

ill / healthy

may sakit / malusog

illegal / legal

ilegal / legal

intelligent / stupid

matalino / tanga

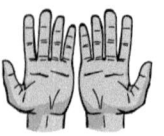

left / right

kaliwa / kanan

near / far

malapit / malayo

opposites - magkasalungat

new / used

bago /gamit na

nothing / something

wala /mayroon

old / young

matanda / bata

on / off

naka-on / naka-off

open / closed

bukas / sarado

quiet / loud

tahimik / maingay

rich / poor

mayaman / mahirap

right / wrong

tama / mali

rough / smooth

magaspang / makinis

sad / happy

malungkot / masaya

short / long

maikli / mahaba

slow / fast

mabagal / mabilis

wet / dry

basa / tuyo

warm / cool

maligamgam / malamig

war / peace

digmaan / kapayapaan

0

zero

sero

1

one

isa

2

two

dalawa

3

three

tatlo

4

four

apat

5

five

lima

6

six

anim

7

seven

pito

8

eight

walo

9

nine

siyam

10

ten

sampu

11

eleven

labing-isa

12

twelve

labindalawa

13

thirteen

labintatlo

14

fourteen

labing-apat

15

fifteen

labinlima

16

sixteen

labing-anim

17

seventeen

labimpito

18

eighteen

labing-walo

19

nineteen

labinsiyam

20

twenty

dalawampu

100

hundred

daan

1.000

thousand

libo

1.000.000

million

milyon

English
Ingles

American English
Amerikan na Ingles

Chinese Mandarin
Tsinong Mandarin

Hindi
Hindi

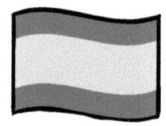

Spanish
Espanyol

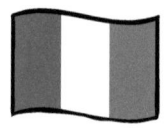

French
Pranses

Arabic
Arabe

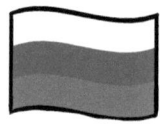

Russian
Ruso

Portuguese
Portuges

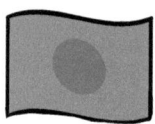

Bengali
Bengali

German
Aleman

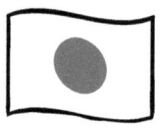

Japanese
Hapon

I
ako

you
ikaw

he / she / it
siya / siya / ito

we
kami

you
ikaw

they
sila

who?
sino?

what?
ano?

how?
paano?

where?
saan?

when?
kailangan?

name
pangalan

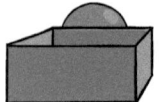

behind

likuran

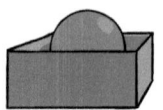

in

saan

in front of

sa harap ng

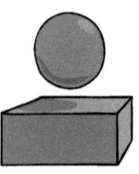

over

itaas

on

sa

under

ilalim

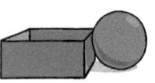

beside

katabi

between

pagitan

place

lugar